THE
Parables of Tracie

TRACIE McLEOD

THE PARABLES OF TRACIE. Copyright July 2020 by Tracie McLeod. All rights reserved. No part of this publication may be reproduced, distributed, or transmitted in any form or by any means, including photocopying, recording, or other electronic or mechanical methods, without the prior written permission of the publisher, except in the case of brief quotations embodied in critical reviews and certain other noncommercial uses permitted by copyright law.

For permission requests, write to the publisher, addressed "Attention: Permissions Coordinator," 205 N. Michigan Avenue, Suite #810, Chicago, IL 60601. 13th & Joan books may be purchased for educational, business or sales promotional use. For information, please email the Sales Department at sales@13thandjoan.com.

Printed in the U. S. A.

First Printing, August 2020

Library of Congress Cataloging-in-Publication Data has been applied for.

ISBN: 978-1-953156-04-4

Scripture

AND LET US not grow weary while doing good, for in due season we shall reap, if we do not lose heart.
—Galatians 6:9

Dedication

THIS BOOK IS dedicated to everyone I know and all the people who have encouraged me in my life. The good, the bad, and the ugly have all made me the woman that I am.

Introduction

MY NAME IS Tracie McLeod. You may not know me because I am not a famous celebrity or someone that you are seeing on television at this time. I am a mother of two with dreams to leave my hometown and achieve whatever God has for me. I have been through a lot in my life, but it has all prepared me to be the woman I am for the destiny placed before me. To whoever opens this book, know that I have opened my heart and life to you. My hope is that this book will touch you and help you trust God harder, and know that your story should be told. No matter what you went through, others have too. You may think no one has had it like you, but they have. Open yourself to the possibilities. We fall down, but we get up. We are not perfect. We were made in the image of God, but we are not God. We will make mistakes, we will get hurt, we will struggle. But, wherever your path leads, just know that there will be someone that your testimony can help.

TABLE
OF CONTENTS

SCRIPTURE 3
DEDICATION 5
INTRODUCTION 7

WHEN You Move 11
IN the Beginning 15
FAMILY Life 21
READY for Overflow 27
BLESSING of Abraham 31
JOURNAL Entry 1 51
JOURNAL Entry 2 55
JOURNAL Entry 3 57
JOURNAL Entry 4 61
JOURNAL Entry 5 73
JOURNAL Entry 6 79
JOURNAL Entry 7 85
EPILOGUE 99

WHEN
YOU MOVE

WHEN GOD TELLS you to do something, He will make sure that you do it. He will send you signs and wonders. At the beginning of 2019, my friend Angela had a vision board party. I prayed over my board before I started. I wanted everything that God had for me in that season of my life. I wanted Him to strategically pick things out for me to place on my board that would pertain to my life now. I have found in my life that God has done so many things that I have overlooked. Now, I realize why this happened and why that person did that to me. God was preparing me for greater. Greater friendships, greater relationships, just a greater me. And, if I cannot say anything else, I will say, "Thank you, God, for all that I have and all that I have not."

The beginning of 2018 was officially five years of me being at my job. When I first came on as a temporary worker, I said I would not be there for more than five years, and I would be retiring by 30. That soon changed to 35. During the first month of the year, I realized the toll that the job had taken on my body. I had worked hours upon hours there, to the point that my wrist was starting to hurt. At church, they kept saying that what God wants from you is in your hands. I kept praying to ask God what my purpose was. My purpose must have something to do with my hands, because right now, I kept getting cysts on the top of them. I was put out of work because I could not do my job due to the cysts forming from repetition. I could do other things, but not what was wanted of me. While I was home, I did not panic. I prayed to God. I figured that if I lost this job, it was for a reason. And if I went back, it was for a reason. I would not starve and neither would my children. I had only about a week's worth of time stored up and I used all of it. Just when I started thinking that I might have to pack my kids up and move back with my parents, they called. My manager and supervisor asked me back. I eventually went back and had to start writing with my left hand because my right was in so much pain. Yes, I had to learn to write with my left hand. It was never as great as my right hand, but it worked.

I did not lose that job, but that whole experience is when I knew it was time to move; because if not, I would lose my hands and my purpose. I'd only stayed at my job thus far because I had just had my daughter and I was not ready to find another job. I was not ready to leave the comfort of knowing what I could and couldn't do to step into the discomfort of the unknown that a new job had to offer. I had to step out on faith and start applying to other places. I was called for an interview. I had only applied for one job, but two people came into the room to interview me. They said, "Well we have openings also, so we both want to interview you." I got the job that I did not apply for. Luckily, I had peace in that place and still had the ability to take sick days for my kids, and time off when they were out of school. Those were all reasons I had stayed so long in the other place. I was able to get that and much more by moving on faith and doing what God told me to. Not only did I step out on faith for the new job, but also for my relationship. I realized my worth and that I did not need to stay somewhere for the sake of having a "family." Family is whatever you want it to be. God will provide that for me. All I have to do is keep trusting and walking with Him in every step I take.

As you read my story, know that with God, all things are possible. In hard times, He has always made, as my friend would say, streams in the desert. I want to give you my life as a tale of who God is to me and some of the things I have gone through. Maybe you can relate, or maybe your situation is different, but know that all things ultimately work for your good.

IN
THE BEGINNING

TO BE HONEST, the ending of this book is actually the beginning. I hope that you will hear my story, receive what God has for you, and grow in your purpose with Him. I thought over and over again if I should write about this part of my life. What about all the other parts of my life? I already know this will not be the last book I write. But this book is needed to heal so many people attached to my destiny whom I do not even know, and some that I do. This book is my life going through seasons. For you, the reader, my seasons will be broken in time. Or it can all be one season — it is however you look at it. Is your glass half full or half empty? I was worried that if I wrote about certain things, it might hurt others close to me. I was worried that they might feel a certain type of way. But the truth is the truth, and they were a part of my journey to who I am now.

Growing up, we lived in a two-bedroom apartment with five kids and two parents. Mind you, I was born in 1985, so my memory kicks in around four or five years old. We were in the projects with roaches and rats and all that you can think of. Drug addicts, women fighting over men outside, bats flying overhead, used condoms on the ground. But my parents saw more than that life for us. Don't get me wrong, it wasn't all bad. The environment wasn't the greatest, but we still found fun in the midst. There was a candy man in the neighborhood. He sold homemade Icees, candy, and snacks. All the kids in the neighborhood would play games together and ride bikes (if they were not stolen). Life in the projects was what you made it to be. There were kids that were troublemakers and kids that didn't know what atmosphere they were really in.

When I was living there, I remember playing with my brother in the kitchen. I had a very small kitchen set that I was pretending to cook on. My brother didn't know what he was doing, and he went into the kitchen and got a real knife. My mom was cooking at the time in the actual kitchen. I just remember feeling something in my back. My brother had taken the knife and stabbed me in the back. My mom took me to my grandmother's house, and they poured peroxide on my back. I know you are probably thinking, *What in the world???* That's what happened. Can you imagine if she had called the ambulance? She would be in jail for child neglect and abuse. To this day, I have a mole on that spot. He didn't know any better and neither did I. All I know is that a kitchen moment turned into a real-life situation.

The most important thing I drew from that memory was that my mom took care of me. I didn't have to go to the hospital. I didn't get an infection. The prayers of a strong mother and grandmother to a great God saved me. That is what I will never forget. The enemy was trying to take me out even back then, but I serve a God who sees all and intervenes on my behalf.

My parents moved out of that apartment complex into a Habitat home (homes built by Habitat for Humanity). The homes were built from the ground up, but my parents had to put in their share of hours in the building process, so their hard work went into the foundation of their home. I was around 9 years old when we moved. I had to start at a new school and leave my friends. It was a hard transition. Margaret Willis Elementary School had plays that we'd sing in. I remember being in the play, *How the Grinch Stole Christmas*. I was one of the Whos from Whoville. I transitioned to Howard Elementary. It was a completely different school, and there were no plays. My old class wrote letters and had them mailed to me at my new school. That was the highlight of my move. We went from linked-together apartments with chaos outside every day to a home with a yard and space. We now had a four-bedroom home. We still shared rooms, but we each had our own beds. In the apartment, we had bunk beds. I remember walking in and them having a house ceremony and singing the song, "If I Had a Hammer." The carpet was clean and movable. We had plastic liners all over the place so that people couldn't track mud into our new home. It was a huge shift in my life and such a great place, just for us.

Fast forward to when Hurricane Matthew came in October, 2016. It destroyed roads in Fayetteville, as well as many other homes and businesses. My parents' block was one of the worst ones hit. Some of my immediate family were in their homes when the flooding started — my dad, my sister Alisha (who was pregnant at the time) and her children, my sister Le'Tisha and my niece Khendal, among others. My aunt that lived next door to my mom was home with some of her children as her house was taken into the water. My cousin and her daughter were at the end of the street as the water came. Luckily, they were able to get out. They had to practically swim out to get to higher ground. If they hadn't done this, they could have died waiting around for someone to get to them as the waters rose. They said it happened so quickly. One second, it was just a little bit of water; the next, it was in the house. My dad and some of the neighbors helped to get them to higher ground. My uncle Chuck came over and was able to get them from where they were to his home for the night. My mom was not there because she worked on the other side of town, and she was at her coworker's home. Of course my mom wished she could've been there to help, but I told her there are some storms that you can't save people from. You can't be everything to everybody, because then, they see you as their god. And there is only one true God. In these difficult situations, you must put your trust in Him and believe that He will truly order your steps and guide you through.

There is a blessing in everything. My parents are both retired now, and they were able to get their home rebuilt through Habitat for Humanity and the other agencies offering money after the storm. They had to live with friends and family for over a year. It was the hardest time for everyone. I was actually supposed to be there that weekend, but I decided to stay where I was because of the hurricane. Normally, even if there is supposed to be bad weather, I try to beat it and just go because I will either be ahead of it or behind it. This trip the Spirit was telling me not to go.

Now I say all this to say, my life has not been a crystal stair, but God continues to bless me and keep me from harm. Not knowing why, I felt so strongly about not going. Had I taken that drive, I could be dead right now. A lot of the roads sank in, and you couldn't get in or out of Fayetteville. God protected my family and me from something that could have devastated us because He is so good. I could have lost my parents, siblings, aunts, cousins, nieces, nephews, everyone all in one day, but I didn't. No matter the storm, God will be with you if you are obedient. Some storms aren't meant for you to go through. If you hear God and listen to Him, you will be saved from the pain of the storm. Some storms you are meant to go through because the pain will birth something out of you. No matter if you do or you don't, God will get the glory and you will see the victory.

FAMILY
LIFE

I CALLED ALL MY siblings to ask how it was growing up with Mom and Dad, and we all had a different outlook because we are all different ages. We were with our parents in different stages of their lives and ours. Your parents are the root of your tree, and what we don't do is ask questions. It wasn't until now, in my adulthood, that I started asking questions about their childhood and how it was growing up outside of their families. Many people may do this when they are children, but I didn't. As I began to ask questions, I began to get answers. I began to get valuable knowledge as to why they tick the way that they do. Take the time to talk to your parents and ask those questions. Why is your mom so extra? Why is your dad so standoffish? You might be surprised by their answers. Even their meeting story will be different because they see things differently through their eyes. Everyone has a story, and you should get to know theirs.

My oldest sister saw our parents through their teen years to adulthood, while the rest of us came into the world when they were already adults. When I came into the picture, my dad changed jobs a lot. I spent most of my childhood with him because he was home, and there was no such thing as paying for daycare. You were with either your parents, grandparents, or an older sibling. Daycares existed, but who had the money for that? My dad would do my hair by putting it into one ponytail on top. Then he'd walk me up the street to get fish plates or to go to the store. My mom was always working. It was to the point that I wouldn't see her as much as I got older. If she was home, she was getting ready for work. Eventually, I realized why. Back then, I didn't understand why she was providing, and stable, while my dad was all over the place after he got out of the military. He had a lot of odd jobs and did construction, but he hadn't found his path. My mom worked at K-mart, and then managed a Little Caesars inside of K-mart until they were forced to shut down. Eventually, my dad was stable and doing well. He finally started working for the school system as a janitor until he retired out as an HVAC worker for them. I learned many valuable lessons from my dad about owning a business, entrepreneurship, how to treat people who work for me, and taking care of my things. From my mom, I learned my calmness, how to use my voice, and managing money. As my dad got older, he started working on his gifts. His biggest gift is landscaping, and I asked a lot of questions that he always answered when it came to his work. My dad has a natural green thumb. One day he planted a garden and everything grew. At my parents' home there are apple trees, pear trees, a grapevine, and plum trees. There is a garden, where my dad used to plant watermelon and corn. When I was younger, I didn't pay attention to those details, but now that I'm older, I do. I asked my dad about planting. He told me to look in the *Farmers' Almanac* to find out when to plant. He told me about what soil to use, along with how and when to cut the grass. It's not until you get your own land that you start to think about those things. My dad always had an answer for me. These are hidden talents that I didn't appreciate until I got older. Even at my age, my dad does things that still shock me. One day, a friend of his showed up, and he started speaking to him in German.

I said, "You know that language?"

He said, "Yeah."

I said, "How and why didn't I know?"

His simple reply was, "Because you didn't ask."

That day, I found out more about my dad than in all the years of my life. It opened up yet another door in our relationship. My dad had never spoken another language around me. He has plenty of work associates, but I didn't know that he had long term friends from his army days that he was still in contact with. That is who my dad is: a person who continues to surprise me.

A lot of people are like that in our world. People have knowledge and wisdom, but when they try to tell you, you don't listen. So they stop trying. I believe that after a few kids, you just wait for them to ask you anything they want to know. My mom always says, "You are so deep." She says it's because I ask a lot of questions and just wonder more about some things than others do. I have always been that way, just not with my parents, and I see it in my children as well.

The difference between my son and me is that he asks all his deep questions now, at a young age, and I waited until I was older. My son asks why he can't do this, or if he should do that. He always wants to gain more knowledge about something. He recently asked me about my parents growing up in the era of Martin Luther King, Jr. Did they get to see him? Was it segregated for them? In my parents' lifetime, segregation was ending, but in my grandparents' lifetime, it was still fresh. My dad said there were still Woolworth's diners and segregation when they were growing up. Black people still had to use separate water fountains. My mom said she remembers that there were black people who still didn't have bathrooms in their homes. And when Martin Luther King, Jr. was killed, some people had to go to someone else's house to see it on television because they didn't have one. I sit back and think about that. The things they have seen growing up and the people they have met. To think that those events weren't that far from now is crazy.

READY FOR OVERFLOW

A LOT OF WHAT happened when I was younger affected my lifestyle now. In elementary school, they allowed a bank to come in and teach us about the banking system. I learned how to be a teller, and they showed me how to write checks, deposit money, and essentially everything about working the banking system. Children and their parents could create an account, and we would have bank days at school where we were tellers and could count the money and the bankers would take it back to their bank.

Everything you do in life has a purpose. I did not search out a man to be my provider. It's funny that men with money always found me, but they had holes in their pockets. ("You earn wages, only to put them in a purse with holes in it." Haggai 1:6). I always ended up being the one handling the finances—their bills and mine. Now I see that men that mismanaged money made me a great handler of it. I was able to juggle multiple accounts because that was the position that I was placed in.

Once I had children, I had to work a lot to provide for them and have a place to live so that I wouldn't have to move

back home. I did have to go back once after having my son due to a loss of hours at my job, and their dad and me not being on the same page. At that time, I was very smart with my money, something I learned from managing the money of my boyfriends. I also learned to be smart with money from knowing what I couldn't have because there wasn't enough money growing up for five kids. I couldn't be in afterschool activities because of money and transportation. I remember taking a class with my best friend Chena to learn to play the violin. My parents couldn't get me a violin, so we shared hers. Eventually, I had to leave the class because I never got the instrument.

I wanted to be in a talent show to do a rap that I had made called, "Get Your Education." Yes, I was definitely a nerd. I forged my mom's signature to stay after school. I asked one of my friends to do it with me, but she bailed on me to be in my best friend's En Vogue act. I still performed with another friend, but I didn't win. I was able to get back home without being found out, but that was the first and last time I would try that.

All those things played a major part in why I am the way I am with finances and how I live my life. These experiences allowed me to continue to take care of my son and live at the same time. At that time, I had joined Insoul Fellowship Church and met wonderful people and made great friends. We were all in the same boat of being unemployed, so we bartered and worked together to get the things we wanted. I was doing homework and papers for people just to get money to do things for me and my son. I was receiving unemployment payments and $50 of child support a month. The child support paid for Pampers and wipes. My friend Keanna had a son in March of the same year that I had my son, and she mailed me all her son's clothes. My son was the firstborn of grandchildren and small children in a while for our family, so he had a nice turnout for his baby shower. I lived off what he got then, along with what my friend mailed to me. I was actively searching for jobs. I was going from applying to be a waitress to hospital work, and then, nothing. By the time I received a job after two years of no work, I was great at budgeting. My friend Cantrel told me to apply for a temporary job. I had never thought about that. I applied, and that was the position I received, so that is where I moved, Burlington, NC.

One of the stories that I hear a lot reminds me of where I've been. This is the story of Abraham in the book of Genesis. Abraham had to leave his country and go to a place God had to show him, and he would be blessed. I had to do the same thing.

BLESSING
OF ABRAHAM

I DID NOT HAVE the typical teenage life in high school. My older siblings had children, so a lot of my time was spent babysitting. I did it so much that my friends thought that I was lying about simply babysitting. They thought my niece and nephews were my kids because I had them so much. Around age 15 or 16, most of my friends were driving and had cars. I took my driver's permit test with my best friend Chena and passed, but I never even got my permit after all of that. I didn't get my license until after I graduated high school because I would have to drive to and from college when the time came. I didn't participate in a lot of the parties and hangouts with my peers. I went to prom with my friends one year, and a guy from around the neighborhood another year.

I dated a guy in high school, and he broke up with me because I wouldn't kiss him. Oh well. I was a virgin and I surely wasn't giving it up. After that, I dated a few guys, but nothing worked out until I met K. We met at a science function. He was on the football team at another school and drove to attend the event. We dated for a while and he ended up going to the same college to be with me. One of the things that I learned from the girls at Fayetteville State University was to not date in college. They said that when you go to college, you will meet a lot of people, and you will get hurt if you try to be in a relationship. I decided that if I wasn't getting married, then I needed to be single. I broke up with K, but we still hung out from time to time.

During my high school years, I remember two major things: the planes hitting the Twin Towers and the war in Afghanistan. We were in history class when my teacher cut on the news to show us the footage in New York of the Twin Towers falling. I did a video report where I recorded different news shows talking about what happened on a VHS tape. I am from Fayetteville, which is a military town, so when the soldiers got deployed it affected everything and everyone. Businesses were affected because so many military families were consumers. When you went out to the club, all you met were military guys. They wanted to party during their downtime, and they needed things to do off base. It was a running joke that when you graduated high school, you were more likely to marry a soldier because that was all you saw, and they were ready to get married. I dated a few and I was proposed to by one, but I turned him down. I was still in high school. I didn't know what I wanted in life, but I did know that I did not want to limit myself and marry someone who I knew wasn't right for me. I would say 90 percent of my friends were going to college, and I was too, so I wasn't going to settle down and marry just anyone. Now I see the same things recurring just like high school. People marrying soldiers and those soldiers being sent out of Fayetteville to Iran. Everything in life is cyclic.

My plan for going to college was because I wanted to go to medical school. I wanted to go to several schools in different states and had applied. I could have gone, but my mom said that I had to stay close by in North Carolina. I had only taken my courses and a few choice electives, but I loved the undergraduate school I chose because it reminded me of high school with the same multicultural group of people. I went to East Carolina University. Before graduating, I had taken the MCAT twice with an okay score. My professors sent off my letters of recommendation, all except for one. My professor sent it late and the colleges didn't accept that. Even though I didn't turn in the letter late, it was my fault because the person I chose did. That made me look bad as a candidate, especially going up against people with higher GPAs than me who had all of their paperwork and references together. I had a dream one night where I could see myself looking at a building that said Medical School and it was slowly moving into the distance. I wondered if I was meant to go to medical school. Why not?

What would I do? Medical school is why I went to college in the first place. I didn't have other options outside of that decision. I didn't want to get a regular job and stay in Fayetteville forever. I wanted more for my life and not to get stuck in the cycle of struggling and never going anywhere.

While all of this was going on, I started working to make money to pay for books and small things I wanted to do. I was able to do a work-study program and worked for a company outside the school. I was let go for stealing a purse, even though I never stole it; I had it on layaway. Yes, I know it makes no sense. Someone was switching prices, and they thought I was a part of that. I said, "No, the purse is on layaway. The tag is on there." They said the person had been switching tags and the actual price was higher. I said, "Well, I don't want it. That's too expensive." I lost my job but they actually said I quit. The loss prevention specialist there offered me a job for a company he worked for outside of that job, so I took that while I was still in undergraduate school.

I always thought he felt bad for me because he knew the truth and what was actually going on and didn't tell me. We hung out quite often after work. He couldn't tell me what was happening. He knew that I didn't have anything to do with it, but that was his job. What could I say besides, "I don't steal"? The job he offered me was with his family. He shocked me because he drove an old, beat-up car. The seat belt went on you as you closed the door, and you had to push down the lock and roll the windows down with the handle. We went to his house and he said he needed to switch cars. I was like, "Okay whatever." Turns out, he had luxury cars, including a Lexus in his yard. He said he did car shows. I would've never guessed that. He told me that the reason he drove the old, beat-up car was to make sure who was really for him. I would have never thought of doing that, but he could tell I was a good person. I liked him as a friend, but he was too old for me, and I still wasn't ready to tie any knots.

A while after graduating (I was the first in my family at the time), I continued to work for the business with his family. His family didn't own the business, but his mom was over it. I stayed there for as long as I could until personal issues from a female in power were too much and I quit. I was picked on for a lot of things that I did that had no merit. I had reorganized the whole office, updated all the personnel files, even created payroll spreadsheets that they probably still use now, if they are still in business. While working there, I met the most interesting people and got a chance to hear their stories. I memorized my license plate because a man came in and said it to me. He asked, "Do you know what this is?" I said, "No." He said, "Your license plate number, girl. Remember that." I have never forgotten.

I went to church with one of my patients. A lady in the church came to me to share a prophecy. I sat in the last row in the back just so this type of thing would not happen to me, but it did. She told me people will not understand me, not even my parents. I told my mom and she asked what it meant and why the lady said that.

I didn't know why then, but I know now. I do things out of the ordinary. I am peculiar and special, so it is hard for people to understand why I make certain decisions and why I am the way that I am. Trying to explain myself can be frustrating. To ask me something and realize that I knew all along bothers people. They think they have a one-up on me, but they don't. I allow a lot to happen, but because I am a person of time, everything is eventually revealed. I may not say something for years, but I know everything happening because timing is best when it is right, not when motivated by anger. I've done a lot to learn the wisdom of timing.

While in undergraduate school, I fell in love with A. He was everything. He wanted to go to medical school at Johns Hopkins. We moved in together and had a townhome. At that time, I was mentoring through East Carolina University Friends where we would spend time with youth and mentor them. To this day, Dy'mond and I are still in touch. We don't talk daily like we used to, but we still speak. Her grandmother was like my mother away from home. What I didn't realize in that season of my life was that A would not be my husband. As much as I loved him and cared for him, it didn't work out. A and I were learning who we were outside of our relationship. We were the perfect couple to others around us. When we met, we were inseparable. He took me on my first plane ride and out-of-state trip. I had never been to Philly. We had so much fun just walking around. I stayed in a mansion with him and his sponsors for the Christmas holiday. We had so much fun — until we didn't.

A was raised by his grandmother, and when she passed it's like he was lost. He changed into someone I no longer knew. I began to change, too; I realized I wanted more. We broke up, but he was still claiming me. People who didn't realize we had broken up would tell me whom he was talking to, and people I thought I was friends with were with him now. It hurt. It hurt more because he was still a part of my life. We still hung out. Even when he crossed over to become an Alpha, I was there helping him along the way.

One time, I walked in on him with another woman. How? Because I had a key to his place. I let him keep the washer and dryer. When I moved, my apartment wasn't set up to house the washer and dryer that stood up tall, so I would still go over there and wash and dry my clothes. I was with my friend Tish when it happened. I was horrified. He literally ran outside naked and told me to wait. I left and that was the end of me and A. I put in my 30-day notice for my apartment and my two weeks' notice at my job once I had two weeks left in the apartment. He showed up the day I was leaving. My brother and cousin Josh were there to help me move. He didn't realize I was leaving, but the memories of the city and the way I was treated at work were just too much. I had to go and start over. I was done there.

Right after I quit that job, I moved back in with my parents. The owner of the company called me and hired me at another location in Fayetteville. I decided to go to graduate school so it would look better on my medical school resume. I got a letter saying that I had gotten into graduate school. When I showed up, there were no classes for me, so I had to speak to the dean. He told me that the committee had said no to me as a student and that I was not supposed to be there. I showed him my congratulations letter and he said, "Well, they can't take it back. Welcome to the school."

During graduate school, I dated someone from high school, but it ended badly. When he drank too much, he was verbally abusive. The first time that it happened I didn't know what to think. He yelled at me in front of his friends for putting lime in his beer. I had never been spoken to that way. My dad didn't speak to me that way, so why would he? I let it go, but that wouldn't be the last time, and cheating would start happening. He started lying to me about why we couldn't sleep together, and I started finding earrings that he claimed were his friend's in the bedroom. Yeah, I was over it, so I broke up with him.

One New Year's Eve after we had broken up, we decided to hang out just to have fun. He took my phone when I wasn't looking and read my messages. He saw messages from another man I was involved with. He didn't know it then, but that man would become the future father of my children. He didn't like what he saw in the messages, and that night went from fun to the police showing up and arresting him on a charge that was unrelated to my physical abuse. A woman showed up at his apartment in love with him and wondered why he didn't love her. So, why did he love me? She followed us to his place from the club and wanted to explain who she was and find out about me. What she doesn't know is that her desire to chase him saved my life that night. I could have died that night. He said if he couldn't have me, no one could. Because she showed up and caused a commotion, the police came on her behalf, and I was able to get away.

After that encounter, I was done with life. I gave up on myself and my dreams. I just didn't care. I started drinking heavily. I was with my friend Shakeia celebrating Wednesday nights at DOCs. I was there so much it was like Cheers where everybody knows your name. I knew the bartenders, DJ, owner, and security. It was to the point that I had a drink named after me. When people would order drinks and not come back, the bartender would give them to me and my friend because they knew our taste. We met a lot of interesting people: NFL players, professors, students, etc. I remember this one night when a lady was drunk and told me and my friend a prophecy. I was not into prophecies then. At church whenever they would prophesy, I would be in the back row looking down and thinking please don't say anything to me. I thought it was embarrassing for the congregation to know something about you. They would always walk to my row and walk on by. Now I understand its meaning. The lady told me that one of us would live through the life of the other. Even after all this time, I remember that. I would always question what it meant, but now I know. As you move and grow in life, you change because your life changes, and everyone can't go with you. At the time, I just smiled and looked at my friend like, "This woman is tore up. What is she talking about?" The prophecy wasn't necessarily for me and my friend who was there; it was just a prophecy that I would understand later.

To write that now makes me realize how much God was with me even then. He was speaking to me when I was lost at a bar, not knowing where life would lead me. I was the lost sheep and He was leaving the 99 to find me.

At work, I ended up in a place where God sent me a message. Even when I had given up on myself at a bar, God sent a revelation through another woman sitting directly beside me. At the time, all these things were aligned to happen in this way. I didn't even know it would make me who I am today. Things like this are the reason why I am strong. I didn't know God's plan for my life, but He kept making ways out of no way. I had a letter from a college accepting me into graduate school that I wasn't supposed to get. I met people there and learned so much about perseverance and hard times, which I am so thankful for now, but I didn't know why then.

I got pregnant with my son. His dad was so happy to have a boy, but that didn't come without its share of problems. He said he needed a DNA test to prove that that was his son. No matter what I said, he needed to know. I guess I get it. I wasn't mad because I knew in my heart what the truth was but for other reasons. I knew that he was his father, but some people have trust issues and find things hard to believe. If I was a man and I was with a woman, I might ask the same thing just to make sure if we were not married. I am over all of that now, but back then? Oh, I was furious. Why didn't he believe me?! Yeah, I'd slept with other men, but once I was with him, it was just him. Why wasn't my word enough? I wasn't a ho. I was so insecure because of what he thought about me based on what he had been through. I hadn't experienced his life, but knowing him all these years, I have come to understand a whole lot more than I did at 25.

When I realized who he truly was, I was more upset at myself. I realized a lot in those moments of stopping by his place and job unannounced and fussing at him. This is why my son is so outspoken; I was all over the place emotionally when I was pregnant. I was a ticking time bomb. I finally settled down and realized that my son had saved me. God saved me by sending me Wyatt. I was going too far into the darkness where I wouldn't have been able to come back out.

He sent him to wake me up and say, "Hey, girl, you're alive. You have a purpose, and your life is not over because one man hurt you. You did not die there, and you will not die here." I was in graduate school, pregnant, wondering what I would do if I could manage to finish. I had a place with my sister, but she started feeling the weight of my pregnancy and didn't agree with the situation. She was secretly planning to move out and not tell me. My mom gave us an intervention. I found out everything, and I told my sister that I couldn't choose her or the dad. They both needed to be in my son's life. After our conversation, she stayed a while longer. She was there to drive me to the hospital the night my son was born. My son was born two days before Christmas. They let me go home on Christmas Day because they didn't want me to get snowed in at the hospital. That night after he was born, I called my homeboy and cried. I cried all night. I refused to give my son his dad's name. I was too hurt. Besides, his dad constantly said he hated his name anyway. Up until my son came out, I wanted to name him after his father. But after all of that drama, I held him in my arms and looked at him and knew he needed a new name. His dad walked into the room that night, held him, and said the name that I was supposed to name him. I said, "That's not his name." He was so mad he left. I cried all night. He never came back. I spent that night in the hospital alone with my tears and my son.

Two weeks after giving birth, I was back in class. I asked if I could postpone a semester and the school said no. If I left, I would have to reapply. And knowing that I wasn't supposed to be there in the first place, I didn't want to chance it. My sister eventually moved out, so I was on my own at the apartment. I lost my job right before my son was born because they didn't have enough hours for me, so I applied for unemployment and received it. I was still able to pay my car note and rent for the apartment.

His dad had his own place, but he would stay most nights with me and Wyatt. He was working and I was in school. I had to pay to put Wyatt in daycare in the afternoon while I went to class because I had no one to watch him. My lease was up, and I had to move. Their dad was offered a job in Rock Hill, South Carolina, and we moved there, but that didn't last long. He wasn't ready for a relationship and was still being himself, so I moved back home with my parents.

At this point in school, I was no longer physically having to go to class, so I was just doing my thesis and visiting zoos and aquariums for research. Through this two-year span, I moved to Rock Hill, South Carolina, back to Fayetteville, then we moved to Raleigh, Salisbury, then to Burlington. In this time frame, their dad moved again and, once again, I tried. I thought the situation would be different because he said he was different, but he wasn't. At this time, I was still searching for a job, and two years had passed. I was living on unemployment and income taxes. I was able to still do things with others because I was very careful about how I spent my money. I was still getting $50 a month in child support. I didn't want to file but in order to get help from the DSS, they were telling me that I needed to have child support, so I filed. I used that money for Pampers for my son along with WIC and food stamps. I had applied everywhere for jobs and went on interviews, but I never got an offer. I even applied to be a waitress, but no one would hire me. The problem was I had too much education or not enough. But I had a child to feed. During this time, I also started to go to another church. I grew up in my family's church, but after attending a new church with an old coworker, I began to love it. The preacher was a teaching preacher. It was a nondenominational church.

It was so much different than what I was used to. I joined a group of females my age and we met up with an older woman from the church and discussed our lives and relationships. It was a great way to get to know people and just have a place to talk about what's going on and pray. I met one of my good friends, Cantrel, through that church ministry. At that time, it seemed like everyone connected to me in Fayetteville was going through the same thing. We were all without jobs, still praying and having faith for God to open doors for us. We were helping each other out emotionally and physically. Cantrel was one of the ones to keep my son when I finally got a job. She was also the one who told me to apply as a temporary worker in the first place.

I had been applying for two years. I applied through a temporary agency and got the call that I had a job offer in Burlington, North Carolina. I assumed I would be there for 90 days, so I just needed someone to keep my son during the week and I would drive back and forth. I stayed with a friend in Raleigh until they had to move. I drove to work an hour to and from Raleigh every day. On Friday after work, I would drive two hours to Fayetteville to go back to Raleigh to be closer to work for Monday morning. I had him stay with different people because I didn't have anyone consistent that could keep him every day.

After working 40 hours a week and driving hours back and forth, I was tired, but that was all the time I had with my son and I was going to take it. I wasn't making that much money, but I made sure that he had food and clean clothes. After having so much stress moving my son from place to place, trying to find steady help to keep him, I gave up. I called his dad and asked to stay with him and drove an hour to work every day. I put in for an apartment but, at that time, I put my son in daycare. I brought him with me for the drive, dropped him off, went to work, picked him up, and then drove an hour back. That got old quickly because his dad and I were not in a relationship. He was just helping me out, so he didn't bother changing his routine, and I grew tired of acting like it didn't bother me that I didn't know where he was when he wasn't with us. I got a call that I got the apartment I applied for, but it wouldn't be ready for a month.

Right before it was time to move in, I was leaving work, and my son's dad asked me not to come down because he had someone there. I just wanted to get my things, but I didn't have enough gas to go there, and I didn't want to deal with any drama. I used what I had and paid for a hotel for me and my son in some horrible place and bought us clothes to wear. After my money ran out, I asked the apartment complex if I could move in. They told me they had just painted and the electricity was just getting transferred over ASAP and they didn't mind me moving in early. I was thanking God because I had no other alternative. I got paid that weekend, so we slept on an air mattress that had a hole in it that I had gotten from my mom's house. Obviously, I didn't know there was a hole when I took it, and neither did she, but we slept on it anyway. My neighbor asked if I had a TV because my apartment had cable included. I said no, and she gave me a television that she was about to give to her church. I finally got my stuff back and set up our new place with just those things.

I went to visit my family and I had no money. I asked for money and my dad said no. I didn't tell him why I needed it. I just left and went home. I wasn't familiar with my father telling me no. He'd never told me no before. He'd always provided. The truth is I never asked my dad for anything, but he was always trying to help me, so this was the first time I had ever asked him for something. It was a struggle, but I wasn't without. I got paid that week and all was well. In that moment, I learned that things were not going to be handed to me. They never were, but no matter the situation, I would be okay. After that, I never asked anyone for anything.

Their dad came up and said he was going to be moving, and I was explaining to him that it was hard to pay daycare and all the bills, so he paid the rent for me. After that, he slowly brought things over. He brought me his couches and other things from his apartment because he didn't want us to be without. Soon after that, he brought himself along too. That was the beginning of a lot of foolish mistakes, but now I know they were just detours for both of our lives. I didn't have red flags. I had fire sticks and burning bushes, but I ignored everything because he was there. He was helping me and I felt like, through all the drama, he would come through for us because he always had. As I grew up as a woman and a mother, I started to change. The things I used to like I no longer did. The hangouts I had with my friends were short-lived because he started to go out more than me, so I had no one to babysit. I didn't know anyone here, so I didn't trust my son with strangers outside of daycare. From the day we met, our on-again, off-again relationship turned into seven years with no real commitment. There were times that we stated we were together in one place and the next thing you knew, we weren't. I was in the epitome of a Fabolous situationship song.

At the end of the seven years and one daughter later, I asked the question: "Do you want to marry me?"

He said, "No, I never said that, and that's not what I'm going to do. You're crazy. You live in a fantasy world."

I said, "This isn't going to work and you need to go." I wasn't mad or upset, I was just over it. Over ignoring what I knew, over hoping things would change, over having kids out of wedlock with a man who didn't want me. I was numb to the pain he caused. We walked past each other in the same room and didn't speak anymore. When I tried to speak, he would get mad and say I didn't talk to him so don't start now. He never stayed home; every chance he got he was in the streets. He cared for our daughter because we couldn't afford daycare, but I could tell he was more and more irritable by the day. I prayed for God to remove him if he wasn't needed in my life. We eventually apologized to each other for the words said in the heat of the moment, but we knew in our hearts that it was over.

I came to the knowledge that he was supposed to be in my life but not in the way that I thought that he would. We co-parent great, but our love is not meant to be. Honestly, we are yin and yang when we are good and monsters when we are bad. He is the other half of everything that gets me, but he doesn't want to live his life that way. I get it now that some people aren't ready or willing to be what you need, and you can't stay around and wait for that. When you are in a relationship, you also discover that what you need sometimes no one else can provide. I was looking for him to be enough. For him to be the support I needed in a new land. To be the best father for our children and be strong when I was weak.

I realized that I was the one that had to be all those things. I realized that I had all those things in the relationships I was beginning to plant in Burlington but, because I was caught up in the drama of my life, I couldn't see what God was doing in my life. It's better to walk away and be the best individuals together. Never push someone to be something they don't want to and aren't ready to be. They are them. You are you. If you push them to change themselves for you, it will never work because they will always revert back to themselves. It's not natural to change who we are. Our passion was natural and so was our pain. We were two broken people trying to find love in each other and not in ourselves and, when we found it, we realized we were hurting each other in the process.

JOURNAL
ENTRY 1

1/17/2019

When I tell you that in week two of this fast I was praying and believing God. OMG. I can't believe it's $95 for the contract to the house, no down payment, no closing cost, all appliances. God is doing exceedingly amazing for me. I'm looking for previously-owned, and He has new. I'm going to look at the property when I get off today. I am so excited. Lord, you are showing out in 17 days what is going to happen for the rest of the year. I can't wait, God. Reveal to me. Multigenerational wealth is here with this home. Healing is here, family is here, and my book will be a movie and will be here soon. Thank you, God.

1/18/2019

I didn't get the house. When I was leaving work, I got the text that it was sold already. I cried. I didn't want to talk to anyone. I told Chandra, Keanna, and Angela, but all I kept hearing was the song, "What God Has For Me." My hormones are crazy since my period came on this week after almost two years without one. I took Wyatt to the doctor and stayed off. They said he just has a virus that is working through him. That's good to know he just needs rest and fluids. I got a few things for Balanced ComPosition, the dance company that Chandra created, to help me stay organized. Chandra got her business cards. I ran into a guy I used to work with.

1/19/2019

Very sensitive today. I'm crying right now listening to Dru Hill "We're Not Making Love No More." Their dad has my charger. I just found my other one, so my phone was dead. I hope I didn't miss any important calls. I got up and cleaned. Queen had a really high fever last night. It was hard to get down. I was up half the night with them and their fevers. I feel like I'm coming down with something, but it's probably just my period. Funny, I ran into someone yesterday and my phone charger goes missing. There are no coincidences in this season.

1/20/2019

Relentless Church. Move in the direction of your calling. There is a supernatural door that God is opening for you. He is asking you to do something and, if you do it, it will take moments, not years, to open.

1/22/2019

I have a house. 1905 Northside. It is being built as we speak. Kristle, my real estate agent, called me today, and the house that she told me about came back. The person buying it made a mistake. We went and saw a home in Snow Camp and then I went to MY house. It's great and, with down payment assistance, I don't owe anything. I had no deposit, no down payment, 0 dollars right now. God works. He is so amazing. I told Chandra, Keanna, and Angela. I want to show my mom when she comes. I have a brand new 2019 home for me and my kids and future generations. My $8,000 down payment assistance will pay my deposit and closing cost, and I may get something on the back end. All I need is a refrigerator and washer and dryer. Thank you, God. I'll write the Bible study notes tomorrow. I'm still on the 21-day fast at the beginning of the year. Watch out for the new season. God is coming. This is crazy. I texted Kristle about that house and another one and said today, "God, I'm not looking at another house until February. I'm done." He said He wasn't.

JOURNAL
ENTRY 2

4/16/2019

BE MINDFUL OF people who catch your mistakes looking to cover their own. Are you a cope-er or a deal-er? You have learned to let people be who they are. God will send what you need to get where He expects you to be.

4/16/2019

I felt like I was in the wilderness for the last few days. Now I am out.

4/16/2019

This morning, my worry was that I have no food for lunch and must buy some. God sent a company to my job that bought the whole department lunch. There was so much food for my kids for dinner and an extra salad for me. God has done exceedingly abundantly above all. God not only fed me but also gave me enough to feed my children. My sign of multigenerational wealth is coming. Thank you, Lord.

4/29/2019

I got several confirmations from everything I heard that God is limitless. I put together my desk, so now the writing is ready.

JOURNAL
ENTRY 3

5/2/2019 – NATIONAL Day of Prayer

TODAY I LISTENED to Sarah Jakes Roberts' sermon, "Pop Quiz." I could not make it to the church for National Day of Prayer there, so I prayed at my desk as I worked and into my lunch break. I cried during my one-hour prayer. As I cried, God dropped a Legoland 40% off coupon in my lap to take Wyatt. My son wants to go there and I want to take him, but financially it is just not feasible right now. But the coupon was a sign to me that soon I will be able to afford the things I want to do. It's just not what I need to do for my family right now. As I prayed, my coworker was cutting the grass at my home (I did not find that out until I was about to go home for the day). He said he knows how hard it is for a single mom and he just wanted to help me out. When

I picked up my son, he wanted to go to the book fair. I forgot that I promised I would take him at another time, and this was the last day. All I had in my account was $3. They were doing buy one get one free, so I used my credit card to buy him books. Lord, I offer you my one loaf of bread to break as you wish. Thank you.

5/8/2019

I went to 5 a.m. prayer and there was a prophecy that something big would happen in 24 hours and 24 days. In 24 hours, I realized that I had no money in my account, my credit card was declined, and my son got sick. Within the same 24 hours, my friend was able to keep my son so I could still work, my credit card was fixed because there was money there, I could put gas in the car, and my children's father came to visit them with needed items. For all the things that I felt like were going wrong this day, God had an answer for every problem I faced. None of the answers came from where I thought they would. You never know how God will work on your behalf.

It also seems that every time I hear a prophecy, it works for my friend. Whatever God says, I have an ear to hear, so I tell her, and it happens. Sometimes God says things to you for others because it is not your time and they just need to hear it. I am an avid worker of the Lord and when I hear something, the Holy Spirit inside of me lets me know, "You need to tell this person or call that person or text that person they need to hear this." I obey because you never know why you are being used the way you are for the glory of the Lord.

5/22/2019

Get ready for the breakthrough, breakthrough. That is what I hear in my head. I have paid all my bills, but my water bill is $23. I have $20 in my account, a $10 Walmart gift card, and $30 in my wallet. No meat, I need groceries. I do not know what God is going to do, but it's coming.

5/23/2019

Well, God, I trust you. I have no choice but to. I have $-150 in my bank account. I paid all my bills but forgot that I had made my car payment and I still have things pending. I have negative finances along with negative paid leave time at work because I had to take off due to the daycare being closed. I thought I would never be in this place in my life again. I am using my credit card for everything else. This is my weekend to write, so I will since I am off for 4 days. I gave a friend clothes from my son that he can no longer wear along with toys for homeless children that she sponsors. I went to Walmart to pass out flyers for dance and my son loved it. He said he likes having his own business. I know he and his sister will own great empires. Thank you, God, for the vision then the struggle. The vision of my book and knowing that I will get it into the right hands gets me through every day. It gets me through no finances, no sleep, kids acting up, no help. God, I trust you. Balanced ComPosition is moving forward, all my friends are moving forward. This is the season of maximum results, and I will not miss it.

5/25/2019

I am cleaning out papers and just found Wyatt's AIG paperwork. They said he did not require AIG paperwork at this time. My son is gifted and proves he is. They do not want to acknowledge it, but he is gifted based on God's scale, not theirs. He and Queen are and will be great in finances, life, and business.

5/30/2019

As I am writing this, I am thinking of multigenerational wealth. I have $-478 in my bank account, one dollar in savings, and other debt, but I am wealthy. No matter what, I have faith that my situation will turn around.

JOURNAL
ENTRY 4

6/1/2019 – MY Car is Not a Trash Can

AS I SIT here and clean my car, I see all the mess my kids and I have made. The buildup of so many things, but I start to clean. I realize life is this way. We allow it to get messy, then God comes to clean every crevice we have. He overlooks the tears we see, the stuck-on food (where we have gotten stagnant in life), and just renews it.

As I brought in my daughter's car seat, it was full of everything, but she kept trying to get it in. Every time I said, "I am cleaning this to make it new," she heard me but would not listen. Don't we do this? God says, "Hey, I am cleaning you up. Just move into a new position so I can place you back where you need to be with something new." But we want the familiar. Even when the car seat was stripped down to the shell, she still would not get out. Sometimes God will cause us to lose everything to give us better, but we do not want to leave the old place.

6/2/2019 — AN Army

As I was driving home from church, my son said, "There is an army behind us."

I said, "What?" However, as I looked, I saw a fleet of military tanks on the highway.

He said, "They are from church, Mommy. Remember they danced and were dressed like the military."

I started saying, "Yes baby."

My son said, "Mommy, I am excited and scared. What does that mean?"

I said, "Prophetically, we have an army. We are fighting an enemy. We just have strength from church and, wherever we go, God has an army behind us."

As we got further along, he said, "They are gone."

I said, "They are not gone. We are just moving forward. They are still surrounding us from the back." Later, we saw one. God speaks through everything, even through kids, even if they do not understand what they are saying or seeing.

6/3/2019

I write my best at work because the Holy Spirit downloads so much to me. I may not physically write it down, but I have it in my memory and write it when I get a break.

PRAYER CLOSET

I heard of all these people praying in their closet or specific places and I never understood it. Why? You can pray anywhere. I can pray at Cici's Pizza. Does it matter? Then I realized I, too, had a prayer closet. At work, it was the lactation room. When I had my daughter, I would go there to pump milk. What I found was that it was a serene, quiet place in my long day. Then I continued to go there, and I would write there. I would talk to people. That is when I realized it was good to have a place all on your own where you could speak to God and drown out everyone else. As I speak to Him there, He speaks back to me in other places. Pray for an ear to hear and an anointing. The Spirit speaks. You just must be still and listen.

RENEWING MY MIND

I am an avid church attendee. I visit and I stream. My church is Mount Zion Baptist Church in Greensboro, North Carolina with Bishop Pierce. This is where I began to realize my spiritual gifts and callings. Now, this is where I go on

Sunday. My children and I love it. There is so much for them in a great environment and they learn so much. Bishop (so many people just say that instead of his whole name) along with the other pastors that I listen to have been on the same sermons. The other leaders that I listen to are at my home church, Murphy's Chapel (whenever I am in Fayetteville, NC). They are John Gray, Touré Roberts, Sarah Jakes Roberts, Steven Furtick, Michael Todd, and T. D. Jakes. This is my live stream line up after I get out of church to just keep the power flowing all week long. This means that never in my life have pastors been in accord. They all preach the same sermon to me. That means that God is getting a message across to many people, but we call to go to different places to be fed. This is the year of maximum results, and I will not miss it. They have all been saying God has something big in store. Be obedient and trust Him. Ask for favor and the Holy Spirit. Renew your mind and check your circle. I began to pray for my mind because I have many thoughts all the time. Mind renewal caused my realization of this.

APARTMENT VS. HOUSE Thinking

I was stressed out. I had paid my bills and forgot to write them down and forgot that I had paid a bill and my account was $-478. I called the bank and they gave me back $72 in overdraft fees. My mortgage was due, and I could not afford daycare. This was my 2nd mortgage payment in life. How could God give me, and I do mean give me, a home and now I cannot afford it? Why would he let me get rid of help and cause me to take off work? Now I am negative and borrowing time. My kids were never sick and now they are sick once a month, and I must take off to keep them because my help is busy. Why?

Then I renewed my mind. I let the bank take my money and there was not enough for the mortgage. I paid my tithes even with what I had. No matter what, I pay tithes because God will take care of the 90 if you give him the 10, and it comes in ways that you may never expect. Then a friend called and said, "You know mortgages are different. It's due by the 15th." Lord, I was getting paid on the 14th. Renew my mind. I am still thinking apartment-minded in which rent was due by the 5th or you would be evicted no matter if you had been there 1 month or 5 years. If I rearrange how I pay my bills and look at my bi-monthly pay period, I can still pay on time and the other things will be paid. God gets creative once everything is pulled away. That is why I was in the hole. I still worshipped. I did not cry, I praised God anyway. He gave me the creativity I needed to rebuild my budget and to get myself in order. I am still thinking too small when God is thinking way outside of my box.

6/4/2019

I have been in a mental space where I have been able to organize my thoughts about this book and what I want to say. It is exciting what God is doing through me. I was on a high from it when I got to work. Then once at work, someone was hired in a higher position than I was that was brand new and I was passed by my old supervisor. The enemy will really try to bring down your mood when he knows that you have joy, but guess what? The world didn't give it and the world cannot take it away. I have mail with me and my children's father's name on it. I really think it is time to close that account and open another one. Maybe two more like John Gray said because greater is coming. I can feel it. God, thank you for everyone you have kept me from and things you have kept from me. Today I am going to write about Abraham, and I will read about it.

6/5/2019

I went through a four-month Bible challenge with Relentless Church. We read Matthew, Mark, Luke, and John. There I read about the parables of Jesus. I got the insight to write my book based on this factor. I felt the presence of God when I read it, and the stories just jumped off the pages to me. I loved how Jesus would explain life in His own way, and it came to me. Write about Tracie in parables. My life is a parable, and my circumstances are blessings. Once you realize the things you go through, God always has a plan.

In 2017, I had just had my daughter, and I was in CitiTrends buying a journal. I did not realize why this was significant. In 2018, I started keeping daily accounts of my life. I had been writing on papers, but they were all over the house. From that time into 2019, I kept on writing. Some things it hurt to read, but it all blessed me from the time I bought that journal. I bought an identical one to give to someone at work that I always see, but I could never get her attention, so I kept it. That is the very journal I am currently writing this book in. I bought it for someone else, but it was intended for me. After that, I went to a makeup party at the church in 2018, and if there was a note under your chair, you won a prize. (Side note: Favor has always been on me; my mom says my grandmother would always pray for favor over all her grandchildren. I see that same favor all over my children too.) I had a note under my chair and won a journal. Thank God for the favor in my life. The same year for Christmas, my friend bought me another journal. As 2019 progressed, every sermon said start the book. God led me toward my purpose, and I did not even realize it was happening. I would go to church or watch a live stream, and the prophecy would keep saying write the book. Do not worry about editing. That is what an editor's for. Just get started. Take that journal you have been writing in and create the book.

6/9/2019

This weekend I had a good time. My children hung out with their father on Saturday, and my friend Angela watched them Sunday, so I was able to work. The money will help in many ways, and this is the last day of my 10-day fast. The first day after my fast, I got to work and the coworker who gave me the most strife was moving away. Tell me there is not a God. GOD DID THAT!

My mom told me that her pastor said to anoint her house, so she told us to anoint ours. I did not do it that day (I forgot), but I did it the next day. As soon as I anointed the outside and inside, one of Wyatt's friends came over to play and Brinks Home Security came over. He told me that he had been trying to catch me since I moved in in March, and with the housing company that built my home, I would get a free month. But he gave me two free months. How about that! As I was anointing my home, God was bringing someone to secure my anointing of the home. God has been searching for me since March to secure what He had given me. This is yet another parable of Tracie.

My questions for God: Who are you going to send to be my husband? I wonder what bank account I will use to open my other accounts for stocks and multigenerational wealth. What will I do when I am debt free?

6/20/2019

I have been hearing things about someone from my past and it hurts, but I have to move on. I wonder why God makes me a part of all that foolishness, but it makes me stronger and it is needed for my life to push me in a forward direction. I have been reading my word every day before I go to work. Monday, I read about Joshua and remembered by this time tomorrow. Chandra texted me. That morning when I got to work, DSS called to get my information about food stamps. I called the day before, and the woman told me I would not hear anything for 30 days from the day I turned in my paperwork, which was that past Friday, but GOD. I got a phone interview that Tuesday and received my increase at work that day. I walked out of work and there was an open robin's egg on the ground signifying that I am free.

Chandra's text read:

I am beautiful, I am smart, and I am a genuine person. I am blessed, I am a peculiar treasure, and I am caring. I am God's gift. Oh, did I forget to say I am a famous writer? Yep, I claim it. My words will be profound to millions, and they will be blessed with what I have to say. I am appointed to God's prosperity and blessings to those who have a calling on their purpose and life. I am that one. I am Tracie McLeod. I am all that and a bag of chips.

As I read this, it started to thunder and lightning. The earth cried out to me as I read it. The next day, I read about God's temple being built. God can build His church on me. Today I read Nehemiah to completion. Israel reached the cities in the seventh month. By the end of June, beginning of July, everything will come together. It is hard right now. The kids and I ate noodles last night for dinner. I took a rapid HIV test just to get the free $5 gift card for food and Pampers.

6/21/2019

I know God can do all things, but where I am right now, I am hurting. I realized that I need to detach certain emotions. There are places I just cannot go. I have barely any food and no money. (I am holding on to my last $300 instead of paying bills to eat and put gas in my car.) All my bills are behind. I just was denied a personal loan from the bank because my score is low. I am hungry, but I have already eaten my lunch, which was one piece of fish. I cannot go and get something to eat because I have to save money to be able to feed us. That was all the fish that I had left with baked beans and green beans. I do not want to go out and spend money on lunch because it is a waste when I need to be buying groceries. God, who are you sending to get me out of this situation?

As I was praying about this, a payday loan company I applied for online called me. I took out $300 to pay bills and pay back on Friday. I cried as I went back into work because the interest on those loans is crazy, so I was praying to not have to use it, but I had it in case anything happened. I called to forbear my student loan, and the lady on the phone was so nasty to me. I cried talking to my coworker about the struggle of being a single mom and the amounts of bills coming in, continuing to pay tithes, and trusting and believing in God. She was saying that I should make sure my kids eat over the payment of tithes. I told her they would always eat no matter what, but tithes is the obedience that I have never lacked.

I may say I don't have enough, but God always comes through. It's just hard right now because I have this big faith in a time where I am really being tested. She touched and agreed with me in that moment that because I have faith God would do it, but He needed to give me physical manifestation so that I could know He hears me. She also asked me about help with DSS, and I told her that I put in an application for food and nutrition and a daycare voucher. The problem is, with the money I make, they still say it is too much. In that moment, my phone was vibrating. My siblings keep a group text going so that was half of it, but when I looked, one of my friends sent me $200. As soon as we touched and agreed, the money was sent to my cash app. Later, before I left work, the DSS woman called to say that all my information was being processed. I went to get my son and they let me know that DSS had called and were following up.

JOURNAL
ENTRY 5

7/1/2019

THIS IS THE seventh month. The month of the completion of God's work of the other six months. The 3rd quarter. God is about to do something big in my life. I took off work for me and also time to write. All I can say is that through everything, I still have a smile because GOD DID THAT!

SHIPS

So just like that, your friends are like your disciples. They are around you all the time and have their own set of problems. I had to have a wilderness moment over the weekend. I just put my phone on Do Not Disturb and spent time with my children and myself. It was the best time I have had in a long time, and I realized how many things

I can get accomplished. You are burdened with life every day, but imagine that times 12 other people's problems. This is what it is like with family, friends, and associates.

Everyone wants something from you, whether it is your time, your advice, or just to listen. I asked God to grant me an ear to hear him and He did, but that same ear is a listener for my friends. When I was younger—well, not that much younger, I would ask for prayer. When they would ask what I would like prayer for, I would always say, "Whatever you want to pray for." I wasn't choosy. They would always pray for my safe travel because I lived and worked out of town (when I was at church in Fayetteville, NC) and surprisingly wisdom. I never understood that. Of all the prayers you could pray over me, why that? I understand now. With everything I've gone through with friendships, relationships, situationships, I have had to have wisdom. Wisdom has gotten me out of bad situations; wisdom is why people ask me many questions. Wisdom is why I am who and how I am. God gave me wisdom in places I should not have been and for people that needed to leave.

I do not understand a lot, but God wanted me to know more for a reason. A uniqueness to just me. I tell my friends things and they say, "Yeah, well, not me. It's not that bad." "Okay" is always my answer. Why is that my answer? Because until you go through something, you feel like you know what someone should feel. I am strong in my friends' eyes. I take care of my kids, I do not sleep, and I make sure they have everything they need. I sacrifice a lot so they can be involved in activities so that they grow up well-rounded and not bored and getting into trouble. One friend said, "I commend you because until I did what you did, I thought you were playing. I didn't think it was this much." I let her know it is. It is a lot; I do not lie. I just do not always say my struggle because only I understand the why and the how.

HOT FRIES

Our problems are like hot fries. We are starving and then we pull up to the drive-thru and our fries aren't hot. Now we are complaining about the temperature of the fries and forgot the hunger that drove us to get them in the first place. We are mad at the restaurant, the people working, and the grill. Then we get the hot fries, we calm down, and realize they are too hot to eat anyway. When God gives us something new, our first thought is to complain, cry, ask him, "Why do you do this? What should I do? How do I change the outcome of this decision?" Once we calm down and pray, we realize that it is the best decision for us. Good or bad, it is to get something out of us, whether it be a change or not. Nothing He does is wasted. It's always hard to do something different, but that doesn't mean it's bad.

THAT NEW NEW

This comes from my experience with machines. We had a machine that had been there since I was born in 1985. The machine worked, and everyone knew how to use it. You knew the buttons to push to get it to run the way you need it to. Everyone was comfortable with this machine because it was familiar; they had known it for years. Why get a new machine that may not run my test? It may not do well. What if we still need the old one? It has problems, but it still works. People don't like transitioning to things that are new. Once the new and improved machine came, it was running smoother than the old one. The test didn't take as long because there were not all those problems. You didn't have to watch it work because you knew while you were gone, there were no problems. Months into the new machine, it started to have the same difficulties as the old machines. Those same old problems were now on a brand-new machine.

How? It's just like life. The machine was new, but it was in the same old position. It was just like us. We become new, but we stay in the same position. So the same problems keep happening. We change our appearance but not our mindset to move into the new place God has for us. He has transformed us, changed us, brought us into a new man, but we still want to remain in familiar places where we encounter the same problems. Like I've heard repeatedly: Faith without works is dead. If you take one step, God will take two. He places everything inside of you, but you must move into the new position.

RAIN

We want heaven to send the rain. Do we have an umbrella, or are we getting saturated with the rain? Do we ask a question and receive it, or do we block our blessing because we weren't prepared for it? Did we leave our umbrella at home or our raincoat in the car? Think about the times you prayed for something and God sent it and then you questioned the answer. God, is this really the man or woman for me? God, I have this extra money. Should I pay this bill? You prayed for money so that you could do something for yourself, but you used it for a bill. Now three more months have gone by, and you have no extra money again. Let God rain on you. Let Him send the rain. You asked for it, so run into it. Meet the rain before it hits the ground. Let God see you waiting on the rain to come down and drench yourself in it.

THE COMPLAINERS

Here is a story that most are familiar with, even me. You ever notice that where there is a group of people, there is always a subgroup of complainers? At church, they may complain about the rules. At work, they may complain about a change. But they are always there. There is the group of people that see 1,000 things wrong and speak to one another about it but never a higher authority. There was a time in my life where I would be right there getting sucked into that group. Once I opened my eyes and realized it, I completely stepped back, took a glance, and asked why I was there. What am I doing in this situation?

These people have complained about the same thing for years, and when you ask, "Have you said something about it?" The answer is no. Why not? They don't listen. Okay, so you are going to complain about the same thing for 50 years and never have a result because you don't open your mouth. Authority. God is our authority, and all we must do is ask Him and tell Him our problems. At your subgroup, let them know, "Instead of speaking in circles with no answer, let's speak to someone who can fix it." Too many times we never go to someone to fix it. We just keep going in circles. Years have passed and we are in the same position because we won't look up and ask for help. Tell me how I can fix this problem. Because guess what? To every problem there is a solution. Like Bishop Pierce would say, "If I never had a problem, how could I know that God could solve it?"

JOURNAL
ENTRY 6

8/31/2019

FOR THIS MONTH of relaxation and rest, it had a very different ending than I thought. I was asked to be in a relationship with the father of my children, and he said that he would give me all the things I asked for and more. He said everything I wanted from him that I didn't even tell him. I told him that I would think about it. I needed to see if he was for real and if he would be consistent with us. Within the next two weeks, he told me that he could not do it. He did not want to hurt me, and it was him, not me. I open my heart back to you only for you to say, "Nope, I am not ready." I was hurt, broken all over again from something that I let go of but was hopeful for again, once it was re-presented to me in a fresh way. I thought of the negatives of the relationship and the entire positive, and still I said yes to him. I was put back into a place of wondering. I still believed God for that love from someone, and it gave me my joy back. I was just happy that he told me he was not ready and did not enter back into our lives and waste our time again.

On the last day of August, I found myself in Georgia to go to a relaxing event. I thought it was going to be about branding yourself and learning how to do it in a relaxed environment. It was relaxing more than I knew. My friend Keanna let me stay with her and her husband and children. It was the best time I've ever had. My children and her children are around the same age, so we had our time together. And when I went to the event, she spent time with my kids. I appreciate her so much for allowing me to do that, and it gave me enough of what I needed.

Danijah was the person in charge. I met her through Instagram after she branded someone I followed. Once I saw her work, I started following her Instagram. I noticed all the work she did and thought to myself, "When I brand myself, I would love for her to do it." I noticed her relaxing event and bought an early bird ticket. It came with $10 to spend along with dinner and conversation. I needed the spiritual awakening for myself. I made relationships with like-minded individuals. We had meditation and an exercise that pushed me to release and let go of what was holding me back in my life so that I could move forward with my gift. The amazing thing was, once I got to the door of the house, I felt a great power outside of it. When I came in, I was greeted by her assistant. When I first saw Danijah, or D for short, she realized she did not know me. She came right to me and said, "Relax, go outside if you want to. Take off your shoes." I did. I met beautiful women all with the inspiration to be more. The exercise I did was so amazing.

When I received my folder, the number written on it was eight. My first thought was about the father of my children because his number of choice is eight. Once the exercise was finished at the end, I had a different outlook on that number. It did not remind me of him but new beginnings because biblically that is what the number eight is. The most spiritual part of this experience, which let me know this was where I was supposed to be, was not her treatment of me or the other women; it was my first encounter with D.

In March 2019, as I was at church, Apostle Travis Jennings prophesied to me when I went up to his table after service to meet him and see his books. He asked me if I wrote. I said, "Yes, I have written for a long time."

He told me, "You are bigger than this place, and that book will get into the right hands."

When I encountered D, she said, "What is your name?"

I said, "Tracie."

She said, "You won a book. Did you get it?"

I said, "No I did not, I did not know I won a book." I never entered any contest for a book, so I had no clue what she meant.

She said, "You do not remember. I mailed it to you and it came back undeliverable. I know it was you. I saw your name with a book. What is your Instagram handle?" I showed her. She said, "Maybe it was another Tracie, but I know I saw your name with a book." I smiled and went through the rest of the day.

In the end, I went to D and said, "Do you remember when I first came in and you were speaking about a book and me?"

She said, "Yes."

I said, "I am actually writing one right now."

She held both my hands and said, "It is your time."

I was in an awakening from her, the place, meditation, and all that God has in store. When I am obedient to God, everything lines up. I received money all the week before to get there, gas from friends, and extra for me to spend on me. The weeks before, I had no money trying to make sure we ate vs. paying bills, but I have always had just enough to make it. I have not lacked. That week, there were miracles every day until I left. God renewed me on that day to be more. He wanted me to know that He sees me, and He spoke through her to remind me of my purpose. That same day, there was a woman there who is on her way to greatness who had situations just like me. She was the first person I spoke to outside of D and her assistant. She told me that I would have a choice to make, but I would have to let go.

On my way home that Sunday morning, I played all my sermons on the car ride while my children slept. First Mount Zion, Potter's House of Dallas, Lakewood Church (John Gray was there), then Transformation Church. Some of my other live streams were not working that day. Nothing is a coincidence anymore. If it's not working, there is a reason for that. That meant God wanted me to hear what He said only in these services. What stood out to me was T.D. Jakes' sermon about the story of Jacob and Enoch, and how our lives can change in a moment by a choice we make. It reminded me of what that woman told me that night before I left. If I follow God and stay obedient to His choices, I will prosper. Something else that really stood out to me was that he asked for new beginnings and said he heard the number eight. The same number I'd just had the night before.

Then I listened to Michael Todd speak about wavy faith and Peter getting out the boat when Jesus said come. All disciples had the same opportunity, but only Peter chose to move. Once again, choice. Peter chose to move, and he chose to look back and fell. But he chose to look back up, and Jesus helped him. Through this event and sermons from these preachers, I felt joy and peace. I still have that now, but it made me rethink the relationships and friendships that I have.

In our exercise, I poured out something about myself to a stranger and they poured back into me. In life, I have developed relationships with others that have not been pouring back into me. I have two children, and my friends out of state will watch them for me and assist me with my needs, while people in the state do not even visit me. I know that I cannot do like I used to, but I at least try. I don't judge what others won't do because I don't know their circumstances. And like one of my friends said, when someone doesn't have kids, their priorities are different. They don't want to keep other people's kids because they don't have any reason to. That's fine and understandable, but one day they will, and then they will see what it takes. Friends are there, no matter your situation, to help you whether that is their cup of tea or not. That's a true friend.

JOURNAL
ENTRY 7

9/2/2019

All in my dreams was the number ten. No matter what someone gave me, it was in increments of ten.

11/7/2019

I cannot be the version of me that I used to be for you so that you can stay the version that you are. We have all grown in years, but every time I get around certain people, they bring up the past or remind me of what I used to do or what I used to allow. But that's the version of me then, and this is now. We can reminisce from time to time about a funny moment or something that was so crazy, but I have to remind you that I no longer live in that moment. I'm bigger than that moment, and so are you. As I grow into this version of me that God wants me to be, you continue to grow as well. I bless your journey as you do. "I'm sorry but not sorry, busy but not busy. I'm restructuring for the business connected to my name," — Sarah Jakes Roberts (Restructuring Sermon).

There have been so many things in my life that, now when I began to write, I realized I have been through a lot. I was birthed with my calling, but I got lost along the way. It never did. It always found a way to come back to me. Once I changed my environment and really allowed that perfect peace, it came back and along with it things that I didn't even know would come with it. I have been pushing this away and pulling it back. Part of my calling is helping people no matter what. I will jump in and help without needing prior knowledge. The problem with that is I help people, and then I go home and spend time with my children and have nothing left for myself.

Even though I envisioned this book last year, it wasn't the time for it. Once I had it on my vision board, I knew this was the year to release what God had inside of me. Once I heard the sermons and knew that God was speaking to me saying write the vision, write the book, the kingdom will need this. God will get the glory of this. So, no matter how I feel, how many people read this, God got out of me what He wanted. My story is told and, as I wrote it, I realized He was always in it.

11/8/2019

I met this guy, and some of the first questions he asked about me were all materialistic. He asked what kind of car I drove, and did I live in an apartment or home. They were not about me personally. I asked if he was interrogating me because he was asking me all these questions about my possessions.

He said, "No just asking to get to know you."

I got defensive. Was he trying to stalk me? Rob me? All those things went through my head, but why? Why couldn't I just answer?

Then he asked, "Is your house nice?"

I said, "Yes and why would you ask that? Who wouldn't say their house was nice?"

He said, "I didn't grow up in a nice house. That's why I asked."

Truthfully, we all grew up differently. I have five siblings and we all grew up differently. We all have different experiences of the same place. "The vision is stronger than the struggle." Sarah Jakes Roberts, "Turn of Events."

11/19/2019 – 77TH Birthday (Number of Completion)

Today is my grandmother's 77th birthday. Can you believe that she is alive and well and waiting to go play bingo?! As I sit here, I think of all the things God has done for me over the years. In writing this book, it brings back the remembrance of things that I didn't realize He had done for me that, at the time, I could not acknowledge. Recently, Danijah was offering classes to teach others what she already knows because she is a natural leader. Someone gifted her money so that, instead of charging $300 for her course, she could just charge $100. I got home after a long month and I was just spent. I was so tired I just wanted to get in my bed and let the kids do what they wanted to do. My phone wasn't working correctly, so it was the Spirit just telling me, "Cut your phone on and go to Instagram right now." I was really debating, "Lord I just want to go to sleep," but I did it, and Danijah was on live. She was speaking about her courses and the amazing person who gifted the money for her branded clients to take the course for $100. She saw me log on and comment and started speaking about me and my book and told me that even though I wasn't a client yet, she knew that I would be and that I could take the course for $100. She also said she knew that all her clients would be millionaires.

One of the ladies whose name is Mia asked if I had time to take the course and I said yes. She said she would gift it to me because after meeting me, she felt that I was a part of her soul tribe. I ran through my house shouting hallelujah. My laptop had just fallen out of my hands a week prior, so I did not even have it to use, but I knew that God would make a way just as He had done for everything else. I was so excited. God was building my 300 like Gideon. He has put me in rooms with people whom I never would have met and don't have the language for, but they understand me and care about me. Who wouldn't serve a God like that? I told my friend Chandra. No hesitation, she said, "Use my computer." I was thinking of who can watch my kids while I took this class, and they watched themselves. I hesitated before the class thinking, "Am I ready for this? Is this what I should be doing? You told me to write this book, and now I'm taking a class that has nothing to do with it." But God told me He would give me gifts that I do not have to help my friend Chandra. I know it's all for glory and not for me, so I was going ahead with it. I could not get access to the class. She was writing asking was I getting on, and I was sending her snapshots of how Zoom wouldn't give me access. I didn't panic. It was Sunday.

I watched my sermons via live stream. T.D. Jakes preached the power of His presence to me. God spoke directly to me. He said, "If you are in your living room watching the live stream, you have to go scared. You may not think this is for you, but it is." This message was confirmation of my hesitation and that I am on the right path. Sometimes we are ready for things but God has to prepare us. I took $1,000 out of my 401K in order to catch up on some bills and get a new laptop. Cyber Monday and Black Friday are coming up, so I will get a good deal. And I won't have to bug my friend for hers, as it is for her business, and I don't want to keep her from her needs.

God worked all that out because I could not have a 401K. She is teaching a new class in December, so I will have my own laptop then. I was able to clean and organize my home over the weekend preparing for this class, but God was preparing me for something else. God has more lined up for me than He is showing me right now, and I am ready for my transition and shift. I'm going to keep writing until it is finished. God is giving me a strategy for every move I need to make in this new season, and I will go with it. I trust you, Lord. No matter what you want to do, I will follow you.

While writing this, I have realized all the things that God has done for me through the years. All the places He has kept me. I give thanks for all the things I was kept from as well as what I was given. I was given a home. When I say given, I mean that. There were no strings. No down payment. Just the fact that I kept up my credit. A brand new built 3-bedroom home for me and my children with a one-car garage. In a brand-new neighborhood with the majority of the kids my son's age or a year younger or older. He made friends with everyone and felt right at home after the initial move. All the parents are around my age, married, and raising their children. Now I don't know what goes on in everyone's home individually, but when those kids are out we all speak to each other and watch out for one another's children. I didn't think that neighborhoods like this existed anymore, or people for that matter.

12/5/2019

As I look back on this year, so far I have accomplished a lot, but only through the grace of God. I have been places I never thought I would go and met incredible people. I have seen the potential in others be wasted and amplified. I am at this point getting ready to vend for my daughter's daycare Winter Showcase, as well as selling popcorn for my son's first dance recital. I am also writing this book, being a mom, daughter, sister, and friend. My prayer is that all of my family and friends no longer have to struggle and realize the gifts that God has given to them. I pray they are not manipulated by anyone else and that they are not envious of what anyone has. I pray that God shines on my line for generations to come and blessings on blessings.

BEAUTIFUL

A man had two daughters and he gave them the world. One daughter ended up being loved unconditionally by everyone she met, but the other ended up being burned by everyone she met. The father gave both the world, but they still had different lives. What is the old saying? "Beauty is in the eye of the beholder." What does your eye behold? You can have multiple children and their lives are completely different because, once created, they are their own person. Birthing them shows you their personality. Their parents, guardians, and peers shape them. Take beauty in this way. Growing up, I heard a dad tell his daughter, "Hurry up and get ready. You're ugly, so no boys will be looking at you." That sat with me until I was older. Even now, I can picture myself in that same room with her, hearing her father say that to her. I had never heard a man speak that way.

Where I grew up, I saw women fighting over men and men fighting women in the back of our apartment, but I had to go into the house. I did not understand why they were fighting. I know now because someone was cheating and got caught. Remember this was in the 1990s, so it was real. I may have seen fighting, but I never listened to the verbal communication that went along with that. When I heard that, I wondered how he could say that. I asked her if she was okay, and she said yeah. I assume he spoke like that all the time because it didn't seem to faze her. My dad never spoke to me like that. He always said his children were beautiful. He might get angry and tell you off when you are just doing wrong, but he never made me feel like I was ugly. He bought me the trendy clothes the other kids had once I got older. He never made me feel bad.

As we grew up, imagine you have five kids and you don't make that much. I make more now than my mom and dad made before they retired from working all those years. I wonder how they made it because it is hard with what I have with two kids. Even through all that, my dad never spoke to me out of the way to say things like that. What I have realized though as I have gotten older is that being an authority figure does takes a toll on your life, whether it be good or bad. You can develop complexes about everything and not realize where it came from. I was always the girl to wear Lugz sneakers, loose jeans, big shirts. My parents would get us two outfits for school every year.

I would match up a new shirt with old pants and vice versa to make my clothes last, and I was the youngest girl, so I had my pick of hand-me-downs. I didn't care about my looks. Honestly, I still don't. Any friend who has known me for a long time will tell you that. They know that I am that friend who they had to "re-dress" when we went out. They had to go and pull out all the jewelry, another outfit, and shoes. Since I knew I was pretty because my dad said so, I was never feeling like I'm all that, but I never held my head down either. I loved me and the way I dressed and my hair.

As I grew up, I remembered high school. My sisters did not want me to go to school looking like a regular me. I was their sister. They put a weave ponytail on my hair and dressed me for school. Everyone was shocked at how I looked. I still had my natural hair in ponytails in middle school and my hair was not long. When I went out to the teen club with my sister and her friend one night, I had on a tube top and jeans. I remember all night I kept trying to stretch that top to fit my whole body because I was so uncomfortable.

In the summer, we used to go down to South Carolina every few years to go visit our family that lives there. On occasion, the grandparents and all the parents and grandkids would go down to Myrtle Beach. I would run out on the beach in my white T-shirt and shorts. I would go and play in the water but I couldn't swim (still can't), so I would come back up. Someone would lose a flip-flop. We would have packed food in coolers and eat that. My mom told me one time, "Tracie, it's hot. Take that shirt off." I didn't want to. She said, "All these women out here are so much bigger than you and they have just their bathing suit on. And it's hot." I took off my top. I was wearing a bikini top. I had tiny abs poking through, but I felt uncomfortable once again. I don't like to be looked at. It was my mom's way of saying, "Quit hiding your beauty. Go out there and have fun."

My definition of beauty was formed by my parents. Now my definition of ugly came from my peers. I remember coming home from the beach after hanging out with someone and everyone told me how black I was. How my complexion was so dark. I didn't think anything was wrong with that until multiple people kept telling me that. I started taking baths with bleach and trying to use a butter knife to scrape off my complexion. I thought that would make me lighter sooner. Then I would hear from family when I gained weight, I must be pregnant. And when I lost it, I was depressed and sickly looking.

My friends were always the ones to tell me I was pretty all the time and I would tell them back. I was with Chena one day and we took a picture at her Rainbow Tea. There was a slight glare in the picture, and she told me, "Oh you look so pretty." And I said, "Yeah, it's because I'm with you." I always felt like she made me look prettier when we were together, but she would always say, "No Tracie, you are pretty." After getting out of my parents' house and moving on, I started to feel insecure about how I looked when people would say I was something other than what they said. I started feeling like that can't be true because my daddy always told me I was beautiful.

That didn't mean that's how I felt. Boyfriends would buy my clothes and tell me, "This is what's in. You must wear this. You have a great body. Wear this. You are my girl, so you need to look like this." I didn't care or think much of it because they bought it, so I wore it. Not saying the clothes weren't cute but, along the way, I noticed I had my own style. And until I saw something that I really liked, I just stuck with what I had. What most don't realize is that I still had a two-outfit mentality. What I had was enough and if you wanted me to be more than, get it for me. But I'm okay with me.

Then when I met girls that became women with me. They showed me their clothes and tried things on. I liked some and some I didn't, and I started to get a style. They would see my dress improvements on my own, but my style has never matched anyone else's. I have always been in that category alone. Working where I have, I tend to get complimented on my style now that I am older. But when I was younger, it was horrible. I just liked loose-fitting clothes, and it is what I had. Once I started to dress for my body, I started to get attention that I didn't like. One day, one of my sister's boyfriends or friends came by. I don't know what he was, but he started playing with me like a little sister and then he went overboard. I told him that was enough and walked off. I told my sister, and she said I just wanted to get attention. So after that, I tried to stay away from their boyfriends. I have even had ex-boyfriends of people come up to me and say, "I should have dated you." Nope, you dated exactly who you were supposed to and that was not me. Keep it moving.

One day, I met someone who was the father of a child of a person I had met in elementary school. The mom and I had never had a falling out, and we were still friends through high school. Unbeknownst to me, I didn't know who he was and we were talking. Then he mentioned having a daughter and said I may know the mom. When he told me who she was, I completely cut him off. I told him why and that even though we hadn't seen each other in years that we never fell out of friendship and that's a line I didn't want to cross. Believe me, I have crossed a line a time or two, but the truth is I did that because I felt that people always ran over me, so I had to do what I should have. That could be talking to someone and then when it got too far, stopping because I knew I couldn't go further. My biggest challenge, which is my biggest strength, has always been lying, and I could not do it. I am too honest, so I either say nothing or tell the truth.

All these things contributed to my idea of what is beautiful. I have never liked attention. I have dated guys who liked the attention I received as an ego boost to them, but then it would go sour very quickly. Now I wanted their friend or their cousin or that guy I was speaking to. I was too comfortable. I've heard I was too flirty with men and women. I wondered how you can be that way, and they would tell me it was how I carried myself. I'm sorry, I didn't know speaking and being friendly meant I wanted a person. Once again, I would go back into an isolation shell of not speaking to people and being very private.

Beautiful is a word we use to describe something we like that's different from something else that we have seen that impacts us on another level. At a young age, I felt that I was beautiful because my dad said I was. As a teenager, I still believed that. As a high schooler, my views changed when boys started coming on to me for my body and how my lips looked. It made me feel insecure because they were pointing out features that made me beautiful as though I, as a whole person, was not that beautiful being that my father said that I was.

Epilogue

21 DAYS

IT'S BEEN SAID that it takes 21 days to form any new habit. What do you think? I've learned this through prayer and fasting. Every year since 2017, I have done the 21-day fast with and without church. What I have learned is it does take 21 days to form a new habit and for God to show up for you as you pray and fast. In 2018, I did prayer and fasting several times throughout the year.

At that time, God spoke to me and showed me something new every day. There was opposition. Did I choose to believe what I saw and trust the process, or did I say no this isn't right and fail on God's love and promises towards me? I thought that this book would be finished in 2019, but it wasn't. What I found was that, in writing, I found me. Through writing, I have realized who I truly am and my purpose. It was scary to know that all my life I have been doing something that I wasn't trained to do in order to get out of my anger, frustration, and happiness. I internalized who I was to be what everyone else wanted, and the only person who knew me was God. There were even days that I would say to myself, "Should I write that down? What if someone reads it?" So what if they did? It's my life, and this is what really happens in it. In writing this book, I realized that the biggest person that I had to face was not my family, friends, or exes. The biggest person that I had to face was me.

I have been around for three decades. I have seen a lot in the few years that I have lived. What I realized was that in 21 days, I changed a lot. I grew a lot. My focus was on one thing, my goals. Whether they were personal, professional, or spiritual, they were mine to accomplish and no one else's. As I grew closer spiritually, I started to think about what I listen to and what I take in on a daily basis. When I was going through relationship problems, what was I feeding myself? What was he feeding himself? If all I hear is couples arguing, someone wanting what isn't there. All that is in your head. Yeah sometimes it's must-see television or a song that's my jam because the singer has a great voice, but what is it saying? When I do, what I see and hear, how will I feel after, what are the consequences of the decisions I make based on the actions I took? The 21-day fast is a process where my focus was on the above, and I found out about all of my distractions and what I should be focused on: my purpose. My story grew from God's thought to my mother and father and me becoming present in the womb. My journey has been long and hard. Now that I have learned about God and the miracles He has done, I walk with my faith. I no longer wonder how or why something is. I just know it is so, and it is well. I used to get so mad and say, "Why me, God?" My friend would say, "Why not you?" I would give him the side eye like I couldn't stand him. I laugh about it now, but when I was going through it, I couldn't see it. I prayed for an ear to hear and discernment of people. I only want those around me that should be and are meant for my purpose.

I wake up and listen to motivational messages from Les Brown, Steve Harvey, Denzel Washington, Tyler Perry, and Oprah Winfrey as I get up with my children in the morning and prepare for work. I hear them speak about valuing your time because if not, you will let others waste it. Time is something that can be redeemed when lost but lost all the same. They all started out just being them and finding their purpose as their lives grew, but they never gave up. They continued to trust God, and they did it broke. You don't have to have it all together to start. Just start. Whatever it is, just start. God will get you to the finish. This book may be one of many books to come, but I had to start.

The end of the journey is the beginning of a new one. Even today, I have been through the highs and the lows. I'm at the point where this is the lowest I can go and — Bam! I get up in the morning and there is opposition staring me in the face. What I found in those times as I cried my tears, prayed, and yelled to God is that He always made a way. I might be upset because I'm not in control, but God always is. That day the car didn't start, He was saying stay home. That day my son was sick, He was saying stay home. My daughter had a million fevers from teething, but she couldn't go to daycare. God was telling me to stay home. He will still take care of you, but sometimes He will use what's closest to you to lay you down in those green pastures because you will not do it yourself. I took my children to stay with my mom and was throwing up sick at work the next day, and all I thought was, "God, you sent them away so I would rest and knew that I wouldn't, so now I have to." Now I listen. Now I strategize. Now I know there is a method behind the madness. But the only one who knows the end is the one who orders my steps and yours. Rejoice in your pain. Be mad, be emotional, then be still, and know that he is God.

It is written.

www.ingramcontent.com/pod-product-compliance
Lightning Source LLC
Chambersburg PA
CBHW071906070526
44583CB00016B/1864